SWANS OF THE TYNE

A pictorial tribute to the achievements of Tyne shipbuilders Swan Hunter

"I have seen old ships sail like swans asleep ..."
James Elroy Flecker, 1884-1915

by
Ken Smith and Ian Rae

Published jointly by Newcastle upon Tyne City Libraries & Arts
and North Tyneside Libraries

Front cover:

The Shell oil tanker *Solen* is launched at the Wallsend Shipyard in June 1961. *(Swan Hunter Shipbuilders)*

Back cover:

The Swan Hunter-built ferry *Leda* approaches the Tyne Commission Quay, North Shields, after a voyage from Norway in 1963. *(Ian Rae)*

Acknowledgements:

Dr K.R. Chapman.
Mr I. Stokoe, Price Waterhouse.
The authors also wish to thank Pat Cook for her work in preparing the manuscript.

British Library Cataloguing-in-Publication Data.
A catalogue record for this book is available from the British Library.

ISBN: 1 85795 021 6

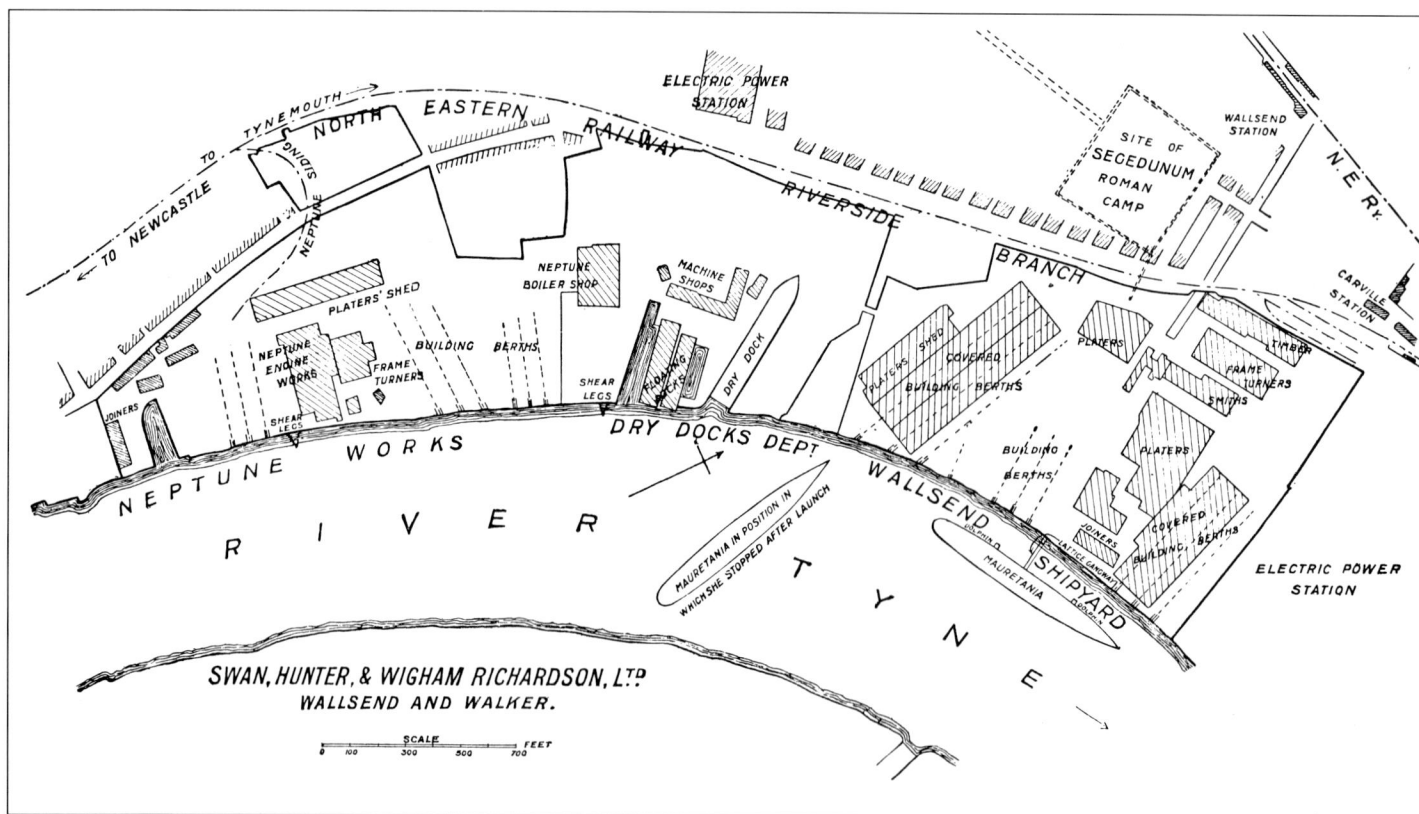

Plan of the works from the souvenir issue of *The Shipbuilder*, celebrating the launch of the *Mauretania*, November 1907

INTRODUCTION

Swan Hunter is one of the most experienced shipbuilding companies in the world and can trace its origins to the year 1860 when John Wigham Richardson, a Quaker, founded the Neptune Shipyard at Low Walker, Newcastle.

The yard's first ship, the tiny paddle steamer *Victoria*, was launched into the Tyne in July 1860. Built for service between the mainland and Ryde, Isle of Wight, she was a mere 65ft long with a 13ft beam. The vessel could be described as a hoof-on, hoof-off carrier for she was fitted with a watertight hinged door which acted as a ramp for horses, carts and cattle to be embarked as well as foot passengers. Construction costs amounted to £698. The cross-Solent ferry seemed an insignificant start to Wigham Richardson's venture, yet the *Victoria* was the first in a long line of ships destined to make the craftsmanship of the Neptune and Wallsend yards renowned throughout the world.

In 1873 another leading Tyneside shipbuilder, Charles Mitchell, set up a shipyard at Wallsend which was managed by two of his business associates. However, the yard hit major financial difficulties and the following year Mitchell appointed his brother-in-law, Charles Sheriton Swan, as manager. The resulting new business was known as C.S. Swan and Company. However, in 1879 the hard-working Swan was killed in an accident in the English Channel. He was returning from a business trip to Europe with his wife and fell from the bows of a paddle steamer, suffering fatal injuries when he was hit by one of the paddles.

The vacuum left at the Wallsend yard by the pioneering manager's death was filled by George Burton Hunter, a shipbuilder from Sunderland, who became the new managing director after entering into business partnership with Charles Swan's widow. The company was renamed C.S. Swan and Hunter Ltd in 1880. It became a limited company in 1895.

Another milestone in the Tyne's shipbuilding history occurred in 1903 when Wigham Richardson's company merged with Swan and Hunter to bid for the order to build the river's most famous passenger ship, the Cunard express liner *Mauretania*. This magnificent four-funnel queen of the ocean was launched at the Wallsend yard in 1906 and delivered a year later. The *Mauretania* went on to capture the Blue Riband of the Atlantic and held the honour longer than any other liner, for 22 years on the eastward crossing and 20 years westward. She remains the largest passenger ship to be completed on the Tyne and is still an emblem of the river's proud shipbuilding tradition.

The amalgamation of the two companies was to prove permanent and brought the Wallsend and Neptune yards together in a highly successful association on the north bank of the river under the name Swan Hunter and Wigham Richardson Ltd.

The decade before the First World War was the heyday of these yards in terms of orders won and completed. In 1906 and 1912 they held the world record for gross tonnage of shipping constructed. In 1907 their output of ships was 15% of the world's total tonnage built in that year. The *Mauretania* was not the only ship completed by the company in 1907. The Wallsend and Neptune yards were engaged on building no less than 11 other vessels in that year. All were merchant ships. At Wallsend work was proceeding on a pair of cargo-passenger liners, a North Sea passenger ferry and two cargo ships.

At the Neptune yard, a short distance up river in Low Walker, the workforce was busy on two passenger ships, three cargo vessels and a cableship.

During more than 130 years of operation the two yards have built over 1,600 ships. The list features most types of vessel, including passenger liners, cargo liners, ferries, oil tankers, ice breakers, cableships, steam yachts, Great Lake freighters, cruisers, destroyers, frigates, sloops, submarines and aircraft carriers. In addition, 35 floating docks have been constructed, including one for Singapore in 1927 which was towed to its destination in seven sections and provided a facility for the refit of British battleships in the Far East.

The list of Swan Hunter customers is truly international, with orders received from a host of countries, among them Britain, France, Portugal, Spain, Italy, Sweden, Canada, Norway and Japan.

The company has been a major builder of oil tankers, not least of which were eight supertankers of around 250,000 deadweight tonnes. These were the largest vessels to be produced on the Tyne. The first of these giants is well remembered by the people of Tyneside, *Esso Northumbria*, launched at the Wallsend yard by Princess Anne in 1969. The company was at the forefront of tanker design until the mid 1970s, completing 46 vessels for BP and 41 for Shell.

Cargo and cargo-passenger liners were once another mainstay of the order books, with 30 being delivered for the British India Steam Navigation Co, 24 for the Ellerman Line and 22 for the Port Line.

In the passenger ship category, Swan Hunter has a fine record, even laying aside the achievements of the legendary *Mauretania*. A notable example was the Italian liner *Giulio Cesare*, delivered in 1921 but wrecked during an Allied bombing raid near Trieste in 1944. She featured elegant interiors and luxurious accommodation as well as an impressive external profile. Also of note was the *Bergensfjord*, launched in 1955 as the flagship of the Norwegian-America Line and delivered a year later. She had an extensive aluminium superstructure (unusual at that date) and provided a floating showcase for Scandinavian artists who contributed works for her interiors.

The firm's output includes the present day passenger ships *Enrico Costa* and *Vistafjord*. The *Enrico Costa* was launched at the Neptune yard in 1950 and was originally named the *Provence*. She currently cruises in the Mediterranean. The *Vistafjord* was completed in 1973 for the Norwegian-America Line and later sold to Cunard. She is now a top-rated cruise liner and was the last passenger ship built on the Tyne.

The Wallsend yard has witnessed the birth of many famous ships. The *Mauretania* of 1907 stands above the rest in the league of honour, but others have included: the *Carpathia*, which braved icebergs to rescue the survivors of the *Titanic* disaster in 1912; the passenger-cargo liner *Dominion Monarch*, the largest diesel motor-driven ship in the world when completed in 1939; and the modern day Royal Navy aircraft carriers HMS *Ark Royal* and HMS *Illustrious*, completed in the 1980s.

The Neptune yard too has been the birthplace of significant ships. One of the Tyne's finest early passenger steamers, the *Alfonso XII*, was a product of the yard's workmanship. This sleek, two-funnel liner was designed by Charles Denham Christie, the partner of John Wigham Richardson. Built for Spanish owners, she was intended to carry troops as well as civilians. Sadly, the *Alfonso XII* was lost off the Cuban coast while blockade running during the Spanish-American War of 1898. She had been completed at Neptune only 10 years earlier.

Another ship turned out by the yard was no beauty but can be described as an important pioneer. She was the *Hornby Grange*, one of the world's first large refrigerated cargo carriers. This mundane queen sailed from the Tyne to begin her career in 1890. However, Neptune gained perhaps its greatest reputation for another type of specialised vessel, the cableship. Twenty-four of these, built to lay and repair telephone or telegraph cables, were constructed. The first was the *Colonia*, delivered in 1902. A 25th cableship, the *Sir Eric Sharp*, was launched at Wallsend in 1988.

Swan Hunter's expertise in producing Royal Navy vessels is undisputed and they were well represented in both world wars. The two conflicts witnessed immense activity at the yards with the construction of new warships and merchant vessels to meet the demands of the war efforts, as well as numerous conversions and repairs to ships damaged in action.

More than 80 destroyers have passed down the slipways, most of them at Wallsend. Some fought at the Battle of Jutland in 1916 and others served with distinction during the Second World War. Among the larger warships built were many cruisers, including HMS *Edinburgh*, completed in 1939 and sunk with a cargo of gold during the Russian Arctic convoys in 1942. The Colony Class cruisers HMS *Newfoundland*, HMS *Gambia* and HMS *Mauritius* were also Swan Hunter-built.

A notable conversion job during the Second World War was the *Port Vindex*, a refrigerated cargo vessel transformed into an escort aircraft carrier for Russian convoy duties. After the war, HMS *Vindex* was converted back to her peacetime role. The largest warship constructed was the battleship HMS *Anson*, a sister of the famous Walker-built HMS *King George V*. The *Anson* was delivered by the Wallsend yard in 1942 and her main role was to provide back-up cover for the Russian convoys.

Recent years have seen the production of a series of anti-submarine frigates, including the Type-22s HMS *Sheffield*, HMS *Coventry* and HMS *Chatham*, and the Type-23s HMS *Westminster*, HMS *Northumberland* and HMS *Richmond*, launched in 1993.

Because the Wigham Richardson family were Quakers the Neptune yard never sought warship orders during its early years, but in the First World War it made a modest break with this principle and built minesweeping sloops and convoy escort vessels. Ironically, the last ship to go down a slipway at Neptune was a frigate, HMS *Chatham*, launched in 1988. The yard then ceased hull construction and launchings, leaving Wallsend as the only true shipbuilding base on the Tyne.

The vessels featured in the following pages represent a small selection of the ships born at Wallsend and Neptune. Sisters of the Tyne, they sailed forth from the river to varied and fascinating careers, some spanning several decades, upon the world's oceans. In doing so, they carried the name of the Tyne and its proud workmanship to the four corners of the globe.

Ken Smith, May 1994

THE SHIPS

	Page		Page
Ambrose (1861)	6	British Governor (1926)	28
Alfonso XII (1888)	7	Inanda (1925)	29
Citta di Venezia (1890)	8	Port Gisborne (1928)	30
America Maru (1898)	9	Knight of Malta (1929)	31
Carpathia (1903)	10	Twickenham Ferry (1934)	32
Colonia (1902)	11	Joseph Medill (1935)	33
Hornby Grange (1890)	12	Sobieski (1939)	34
Albion (1904)Ian Rae Collection	13	HMS Edinburgh (1939)	35
Mauretania (1907)	14-15	Dominion Monarch (1939)	36
Ocean Prince (1907)	16	HMS Tartar (1939)	37
Afrique (1908)	17	HMS Vindex (1943)	38
Acajutla (1911)	18	Gothic (1948)	39
HMS Shark (1913)	19	Velutina (1950)Ian Rae Collection	40
San Fraterno (1913)	20	Leda (1953)Ian Rae Collection	41
Karoa (1915)	21	Bergensfjord (1956)	42
Giulio Cesare (1921)	22	Clan Finlay (1962)	43
Monarch (1916)	23	Lobito Palm (1960)	44
HMS Coventry (1918)	24	Vistafjord (1973)Ian Rae Collection	45
HMS L5 (1918)	25	HMS Bristol (1973)Ian Rae Collection	46
HMS Whirlwind (1918)	26	Esso Northumbria (1970)Ian Rae Collection	47
Meduana (1922)	27	HMS Ark Royal (1985)	48

All photographs are from the collection of Swan Hunter Shipbuilders unless otherwise indicated. Where possible the photographer is acknowledged.

Ambrose

(Completed 1861, Neptune yard). This sailing vessel was the second ship to be built at Neptune, serving on the Liverpool-India route. In 1885 she was sold to A. Weir of Glasgow, and renamed *Willowbank*. This began the tradition of all Weir's ships bearing the suffix 'bank'. *Willowbank* was lost when she was in collision with an American steamer in December 1895.

Alfonso XII

(Completed 1888, Neptune yard). At the time of her completion this impressive-looking passenger ship was the pride of the Tyne. The twin daughters of the ship's captain carried out the launching ceremony by breaking two bottles of champagne over her bows. The Neptune yard was so proud of its luxurious new liner that after completion she was moved down river to Jarrow Slake where she was opened for public viewing. Tickets to see the *Alfonso XII* cost one shilling each. The money raised was given to Whitley Bay Convalescent Homes. Built for Spanish owners, she was intended to serve as a troopship as well as a civilian passenger vessel. One of her main routes was between Spain and Cuba, but she also did runs to Manila and New York. However, the career of the *Alfonso XII* was brought to a sudden and premature end during the Spanish American War of 1898. In July of that year she attempted to evade the American blockade of Cuba and enter Havana harbour, but she was chased by an armed US patrol yacht and made westwards along the Cuban coast at high speed. The liner then tried to enter Port Mariel harbour, but ran aground on a reef near the entrance. The helpless *Alfonso XII* was then devastated by gunfire from American warships, becoming a total wreck. Most of her crew, passengers and troops escaped in lifeboats before the bombardment.

Citta di Venezia is seen lying in the Albert Edward Dock, North Shields, prior to delivery.

Citta di Venezia

(Completed 1890, Neptune yard). A passenger ship with accommodation for 1,177, she was originally built to carry emigrants from Europe to the United States. Her first owners went bankrupt and after a spell under the Dutch flag she was sold to the Chilean Navy in 1896 as a transport. The ship was rebuilt in 1925 as a fleet collier. In July 1928 the vessel sailed from Punta Arenas in Chile with 215 crew and 76 passengers but encountered a gale and fog, running aground at Punta Marquillas. Only 12 were saved.

America Maru

(Completed 1898, Wallsend yard). She was built for a Japan-San Francisco mail and passenger service. During the Russo-Japanese War of 1904-05 she served as a fleet despatches vessel, later being transferred to Japanese inter-island routes. During the Second World War *America Maru* was used as a transport and in 1944 was torpedoed and sunk by the US submarine *Nautilus* while carrying 1,500 plantation workers.

Carpathia

(Completed 1903, Wallsend yard). Built for transatlantic service, the Cunard passenger liner *Carpathia* became famous when she rescued over 700 survivors of the *Titanic* disaster in April 1912. She had sailed at full steam for 58 miles to reach the *Titanic*'s last reported position, encountering icebergs on the way. As dawn broke on April 15 she began picking up the survivors from the lifeboats. *Carpathia* landed them safely at New York. Ironically, she too met her end in the North Atlantic when she was torpedoed by a U-boat on July 17, 1918, while on a voyage from Liverpool to the USA. She sank with the loss of five lives. The survivors were rescued by a minesweeping sloop. Her engines, which served her particularly well during her *Titanic* mercy mission, were built by the Wallsend Slipway and Engineering Co Ltd. Prior to the First World War she served mainly on the Mediterranean-New York service.

Colonia

(Completed 1902, Neptune yard). At the time of her completion she was the world's largest cable ship. *Colonia* laid a cable between Vancouver and Australia. In 1928 she was converted into a whale factory ship for Norwegian owners. By 1937 she had changed hands again, this time flying the German flag but still in the whaling trade. The ship was sunk by Russian aircraft in 1944 while acting as a transport.

Hornby Grange

(Completed 1890, Neptune yard). The twin-funnelled *Hornby Grange* was one of the largest refrigerated cargo ships of her day. She was built for Houlder Line's South America run.

In July 1918 the *Hornby Grange* was attacked in the English Channel by a U-boat. She survived and was sold to Spanish owners in 1919. The vessel was broken up in 1928.

This rare photograph shows Albion *in hospital livery at Southampton.*

Albion

(Completed 1904, Wallsend yard). *Albion* was an elegant turbine-powered steam yacht which cost £64,055 to build, a considerable sum in Edwardian times. During the First World War she was used as a hospital ship, being equipped with 46 beds. Later, *Albion* served as an auxiliary patrol yacht based at Larne in Northern Ireland. During this spell of duty she picked up the 112 survivors of the P & O steamer *Peshawar*, which had been torpedoed off Ireland. In 1930 *Albion* was sold to millionaire Sir Thomas Lipton, who renamed her *Erin* and used her as his base ship during his last attempt to win the America's Cup. She was broken up in 1936.

Frank & Sons, South Shields

A great ship is born – Mauretania *is pictured at her launch in 1906.*

Mauretania

(Completed 1907, Wallsend yard). The Tyne's largest and most famous passenger ship was built for Cunard's transatlantic express service between Britain and the United States. *Mauretania* (31,938 gross tons) was launched by the Dowager Duchess of Roxburghe on September 20, 1906. On her maiden voyage from Liverpool to New York in November 1907 a storm prevented her capturing the Blue Riband on the westward passage. But on the home run eastward she won the honour with a speed of 23.69 knots. In May 1908 *Mauretania* broke the record for the westward run. However, in July of that year *Lusitania*, her sister, won the westward record back. *Mauretania* finally regained the honour in September 1909 with a speed of 26.06 knots. She retained the westward record for 20 years and the eastward for 22, until beaten by the German liner *Bremen* in 1929.

Mauretania *on official trials in the Autumn of 1907.*

During the First World War the Tyne's best-loved liner served as a troop carrier and also did a brief spell as a hospital ship. After the war she returned to the transatlantic run. In her final years, from 1930 onwards, she became a cruise liner, visiting such areas as the Mediterranean and the West Indies. On her voyage to the breaker's yard at Rosyth in 1935 *Mauretania* halted off the mouth of the Tyne to say farewell to the hard-working people who had built her, firing rockets in salute to the river where she was born. Her powerful turbine engines had been constructed by the Wallsend Slipway and Engineering Co Ltd to the designs of brilliant Tyneside inventor Sir Charles Parsons.

Frank & Sons, South Shields

Ocean Prince

(Completed 1907, Wallsend yard). A typical cargo ship of her day, she was built for Tyneside shipowner Sir James Knott's Prince Line. The vessel broke adrift while fitting out at Wallsend, the repairs costing £3,360. While bound for Rotterdam in 1909 *Ocean Prince* became disabled in a south-westerly gale and had to be towed the 30 miles into port. During the First World War she ran between Canada and the French Channel ports, bringing ammunition and other supplies to the Allies. She was wrecked in the Bay of Biscay in 1916 while carrying grain from Nova Scotia to Europe.

Frank & Sons, South Shields

Afrique

(Completed 1908, Wallsend yard). One of a series of liners built by Swan Hunter and Wigham Richardson for various French owners. In January 1920 she developed engine trouble in the Bay of Biscay while outward bound for West Africa. A north-westerly gale was blowing and because of the conditions ships standing by were unable to give assistance. The *Afrique* was driven by the gale on to rocks about 50 miles from La Rochelle and later sank. Only 32 people were saved from the 585 passengers and crew.

In this fine view Acajutla *is on her speed trials.*

Acajutla

(Completed 1911, Neptune yard). One of a pair of ships built for the Salvador Railway Company, to provide a "feeder" service between Salina Cruz in Mexico and Salvador's main port. She was sold to the Pacific Steam Navigation Company in 1915 for use on a fortnightly Central American service via the Panama Canal. During the Second World War *Acajutla* served as a supply ship to US naval outposts in the Galapagos Islands. She passed into Greek ownership in 1946, but by 1952 had been sold to a Yemeni company. The ship continued to trade in the Red Sea area until broken up in Italy in 1960 after a varied career.

Frank & Sons, South Shields

Shark photographed on speed trials.

HMS *Shark*

(Completed 1913, Wallsend yard). A torpedo-boat destroyer, she was attached to the 4th Destroyer Flotilla at the Battle of Jutland in 1916. During an attack on a group of German light cruisers in the battle, *Shark* came under concentrated shell fire, which put her out of action. She was quickly pounded into a floating wreck, but two guns continued to fire. Commander Loftus Jones, the destroyer's captain, had one of his legs shot away. However, he encouraged his men to fight on with great gallantry. A German destroyer eventually torpedoed and sank *Shark*. There were only six survivors out of a crew of 92. Commander Jones was awarded a posthumous VC.

Frank & Sons, South Shields

San Fraterno

(Completed 1913, Wallsend yard). *San Fraterno* was one of a series of tankers built on the Tyne for the Eagle Oil Transport Co Ltd *San Fraterno*, which could carry 15,700 tons of oil, was the largest tanker in the world when launched on February 22 1913. Early in 1917 the ship struck a mine in the Firth of Forth, but was beached and repaired. Six years later the vessel again survived when she was in collision with a French liner in the River Plate. She met her end in 1927 when she hit rocks and sank off Cape Horn while on passage from Buenos Aires to California. At that date tankers were not allowed through the Panama Canal.

Frank & Sons, South Shields

Karoa

(Completed 1915, Neptune yard). Built for the British India Steam Navigation Company, *Karoa* was typical of a vast fleet running services throughout the British Empire. She had been constructed for the Bombay-East Africa run, but upon completion was requisitioned as a troopship for most of the remainder of the First World War. In 1919 she was returned to the owners who used her on the intended route. From 1932 *Karoa* was switched to the Calcutta-Singapore run. During the Second World War the vessel was converted into a hospital ship and while serving in this role was attacked by bomber aircraft as she lay off Oran, North Africa, in November 1942. But *Karoa* survived the attack and at the end of the war was placed on the Calcutta-Rangoon-Singapore service. In 1950 the ship was broken up at Bombay after a life in which she had served well during war and peace.

Frank & Sons, South Shields

This excellent bow-on shot was taken on Giulio Cesare's *trials.*

Giulio Cesare

(Completed 1921, Wallsend yard). This elegant Italian passenger liner was laid down in January 1914, but work on her was delayed because of the outbreak of the First World War. On her trials off St Abb's Head, north of Berwick, she achieved a speed of 19.5 knots, being the first Italian liner with turbine engines. Built for the Navigazione Generale Italiana of Genoa, she sailed on her maiden voyage from Genoa via Naples to Buenos Aires in May 1922. The *Giulio Cesare*'s career was abruptly ended in September 1944 when the ship was badly damaged during an Allied air raid near Trieste. She was hit by rockets fired by South African Beaufighter aircraft while she was anchored in the Gulf of Muggia. It was a sad ending to one of the finest liners built on the Tyne.

H.M.T.S. "MONARCH".

Monarch

(Completed 1916, Neptune yard). One of the yard's smaller cable repair ships, *Monarch*'s main role was maintenance of cables around the coast of Britain for the General Post Office. In 1944 she was shelled in error by American destroyers. All the crew on the open decks were killed. After being repaired, she put to sea only to hit a mine off Southwold, Suffolk, in 1945. The wreck was bought in 1988 as a wedding gift – the happy couple were amateur scuba divers.

HMS *Coventry*

(Completed 1918, Wallsend yard). This cruiser served in the Baltic during the closing stages of the First World War. Between the wars she was mainly stationed in the Mediterranean. In December 1940 *Coventry* was torpedoed in the bows by an Italian submarine. The ship had to steam back to Alexandria for repairs stern first. A new bow section was fitted in just 13 days. She returned to sea for trials but to the consternation of all concerned the new bow fell off. *Coventry* was again repaired and resumed service. She was finally lost when bombed by German and Italian aircraft off Tobruk in 1942.

The L5 is shown lying between the Tyne piers.

HMS *L5*

(Completed 1918, Wallsend yard). It is not generally known that the Wallsend yard produced five submarines during the First World War. They were based at Blyth and Devonport on routine patrols. *L5* also spent nine years on the Far East Station and during this period her base was Hong Kong. On her return to British waters in 1929 the submarine was in collision with a dredger while exercising in the Solent. She was broken up a year later.

Frank & Sons, South Shields

HMS Whirlwind *near the mouth of the Tyne in March 1918.*

HMS *Whirlwind*

(Completed 1918, Wallsend yard). Typical of the numerous similar destroyers built during the First World War, this little ship took part in the Zeebrugge raid in 1918 and later served in the Baltic. As war clouds gathered for a second time the 'W' Class destroyer was given a major refit for service as a convoy escort based at Liverpool during the Battle of the Atlantic. HMS *Whirlwind* became one of the battle's many victims when she was sunk by the U-boat *U-34* in July 1940 while south west of Ireland.

Frank & Sons, South Shields

Meduana

(Completed 1922, Wallsend yard). One of a pair of French liners built for the South America service. While being fitted out at Wallsend in November 1920 a fire broke out in *Meduana*'s forehold. Due to the amount of water pumped into the ship by the fire brigade and the loose machinery and fittings the ship capsized. Two workers lost their lives. The hulk blocked the slipway where the Cunard liner *Laconia* was due to be launched. *Meduana* was raised but did not enter service until November 1922. In August 1940 she was seized by the Germans at Bordeaux. She was then earmarked as a troop carrier for Operation Sealion – the invasion of Britain. But with the cancellation of the invasion *Meduana* became an accommodation ship. Recovered after the war at Kiel she was refitted and resumed her peacetime service. The vessel did not go to the breaker's yard until 1955.

British Governor

(Completed 1926, Neptune yard). One of more than 50 oil tankers built for the British Tanker Co Ltd, whose funnel colours were a familiar sight on the Tyne as their huge fleet was largely born or repaired on the river. With a carrying capacity of 10,224 tons, she was powered by Neptune-built engines. *British Governor* achieved a speed of 11.56 knots on trials off Newbiggin, Northumberland.

During the Second World War she was deployed on the Arctic convoys to Russia. In April 1943 the tanker was attacked, bombed and damaged by German aircraft while lying at the Mishukov anchorage, Kola Inlet. Repaired after the war, she returned to her mercantile role and was eventually broken up at Osaka in 1953.

Inanda displays her impressive looks in this view.

Inanda

(Completed 1925, Wallsend yard). This cargo-passenger liner was constructed for T. & J. Harrison's West Indies service. She could carry 91 passengers, a crew of 62 and 7,000 tons of cargo. In September 1940 she was bombed and sunk along with her sister ship, the Wallsend-built *Inkosi*, at London Docks. *Inanda* was raised and repaired but her passenger accommodation was removed. She was then renamed *Empire Explorer*. However, the ship was not to survive the Second World War. On July 8 1942 *Inanda* was torpedoed by the U-boat *U-575* off Trinidad. All but three of her crew were picked up 12 hours later.

Port Gisborne

(Completed 1928, Wallsend yard). Many ships were built on the Tyne for the Port Line and this vessel, like her sisters, was mainly engaged in taking general cargo out to Australia and New Zealand and returning to Britain with lamb in her refrigerated holds. *Port Gisborne*'s launch was unusual as the ceremony was broadcast on BBC Radio's Home Service on April 30 1927. She was lost in the Battle of the Atlantic on October 11 1940 when torpedoed and sunk by a U-boat 350 miles south west of Ireland. 26 of her crew lost their lives.

"KNIGHT OF MALTA".
MAIL & PASSENGER STEAMER
BUILT BY SWAN, HUNTER, & WIGHAM RICHARDSON, LTD.
NEPTUNE WORKS. NEWCASTLE-ON-TYNE.
FOR CASSAR CO. LTD., MALTA.

J.H. Cleet, South Shields

Knight of Malta

(Completed 1929, Neptune yard). A fine-looking passenger and mail ferry, her peacetime role was the run between Malta and Sicily. During the Second World War she was used as the mail ship on the route from Malta to Alexandria, bringing news from home to the British troops fighting in Egypt. *Knight of Malta* was also used as a supply ship along the North African coast, taking stores and medical equipment to advance troop bases. She also brought back POWs to Alexandria. The ferry's career was abruptly ended in 1941 while she was on one of her clandestine supply voyages. The little ship ran aground near Sidi Barrani, Egypt, after straying too far inshore while trying to avoid U-boats. The wreck of the *Knight* was still there in 1950.

J.H. Cleet, South Shields

Twickenham Ferry

(Completed 1934, Neptune yard). She was one of three train ferries built for the Dunkirk cross-Channel link in the mid-1930s. The trio gave tremendous service in war and peace. They laid floating mines during the Second World War and had huge structures added to their afterdecks for unloading locomotives and rolling stock at the jetties of mainland Europe following the Normandy landings in 1944. *Twickenham Ferry* was the first Allied merchant ship to enter Cherbourg in that year – she was carrying 12 locomotives and a number of goods vehicles. After the war she and her sisters, *Hampton Ferry* and *Shepperton Ferry*, returned to their cross-Channel train duties. They went to the breakers in the early 1970s.

Star Photos, Perth

Joseph Medill

(Completed 1935, Wallsend yard). Swan Hunter delivered over 50 small, two-hold, grain carriers that ran on the Great Lakes of North America between the two World Wars. These workhorses of freshwater had long and varied careers – all, except the *Joseph Medill*. She left the Tyne in the summer of 1935 and was loaded with 2,784 tons of coal at Leith for her delivery voyage to Montreal. She was sighted off the north coast of Scotland on August 17, just before a severe storm struck the area. The ship was never seen again. She and her crew had vanished without trace.

"SOBIESKI"
YARD No. 1572
TWIN SCREW MOTOR PASSENGER LINER BUILT IN 1939
FOR THE GDYNIA-AMERICAN SHIPPING LINES LTD., POLAND
SPEED 17 KNOTS

Sobieski

(Completed 1939, Neptune yard). This passenger liner was built for a Polish shipping company's Baltic-South America service, but on the outbreak of the Second World War she was requisitioned by the British. *Sobieski* gave outstanding service, mainly as a troopship fitted out with landing craft. She was involved in operations at St Nazaire, Harstad, Oran, Madagascar, Anzio, Salerno and many more. In 1947-49 the liner was chartered to take large numbers of displaced Europeans to a new life in the USA. Withdrawn from service in 1950, she was sold to the Soviet Union and placed on a ferry service in the Black Sea. *Sobieski* sailed on occasional runs to Cuba with Soviet troops during the 1960s. After a varied career lasting 35 years she was broken up in Italy.

HMS *Edinburgh*

(Completed 1939, Wallsend yard). The cruiser *Edinburgh* was launched into the Tyne in March 1938. Carrying 12 six-inch guns in four turrets, she served in the Mediterranean during the early stages of the Second World War and also took part in the hunt for the *Bismarck* in 1941. The following year she was assigned to Russian Arctic convoy duties and was loaded with a consignment of Soviet gold bars at Murmansk. The gold bullion was a payment for the military equipment which the Western Allies had supplied to the Soviet Union to sustain its battle against the Germans. But after leaving Murmansk bound for Iceland, *Edinburgh* was attacked by U-boat *U-456* and was hit amidships and aft by torpedoes. She received extensive damage and there were many casualties. The crippled ship was later attacked by a flotilla of German destroyers. With only one or two guns left working, the Tyne-built cruiser managed to score a hit on one of these destroyers. The badly damaged *Edinburgh* later sank. A deliberately-fired British torpedo had ended her suffering. Most of the gold cargo was recovered from the wreck by a diving team using high-tech equipment in 1981.

Frank & Sons, South Shields

Dominion Monarch

(Completed 1939, Wallsend yard). Built for Shaw Savill and Albion's service from London and Southampton to New Zealand, *Dominion Monarch* was at 27,155 gross tons the third largest passenger liner to be launched on the Tyne. During the Second World War she served as a troopship and her six huge cargo holds carried vital food supplies. In 1947 the liner returned to the Wallsend yard for a post-war refit and in December 1948 resumed service on the Britain-New Zealand route. In 1962 *Dominion Monarch* was sold to a Japanese company and in the same year she was used as a hotel ship at the World Fair in Seattle, USA. Afterwards, she sailed on her last voyage to a breaker's yard in Japan.

J.H. Cleet, South Shields

HMS Tartar *leaving the Tyne.*

HMS *Tartar*

(Completed 1939, Wallsend yard). A dashing Tribal Class destroyer of the Second World War, *Tartar* achieved a speed of just over 36 knots on her trials. She was attached to the Home Fleet in the early part of the war and saw action in the Faroes, the Arctic convoys, and took part in the hunt for the *Bismarck*. In 1942 she was part of the convoy escort sent to relieve the siege of Malta. The following year she was involved in operations off Sicily, in the Messina Straits and off Salerno, adding several more successful engagements with the enemy to her record. *Tartar* was broken up at Newport in 1948.

Philipson Studios, Newcastle upon Tyne

HMS Vindex *shortly before her conversion back to a cargo ship and (inset) her final appearance.*

HMS *Vindex*

(Completed 1943, Wallsend yard). Laid down in July 1942 as a refrigerated cargo ship, this vessel was bought off the stocks and converted into an auxiliary aircraft carrier. HMS *Vindex* served most of her wartime career on the arduous Russian convoys to Murmansk. She finished her war service in the Far East with the Pacific Fleet. The vessel was later sold to the Port Line who renamed her *Port Vindex*. In 1948 the ship returned to the Tyne for conversion back to her original role by Swan Hunter. She served in the wool and butter trade between Australia, New Zealand and Britain until broken up in Taiwan in 1971.

Philipson Studios, Newcastle upon Tyne

Gothic

(Completed 1948, Wallsend yard). A passenger-cargo liner, *Gothic* was built for Shaw Savill and Albion Line's UK-New Zealand service via the Panama Canal. In March 1951 it was announced that the ship would be used as a royal yacht for King George VI's visit to Australasia. She was converted to her royal role at Liverpool, but because of the King's poor health the tour party, and itinerary, were changed. *Gothic* was waiting at Mombasa, Kenya, to pick up Princess Elizabeth and the Duke of Edinburgh when the King died. The tour was cancelled. The ship resumed her passenger-cargo trade until 1953 when she was refitted as a royal yacht once more – this time for the

Queen's three-month Commonwealth tour, which proved a huge success. The *Gothic*'s captain was knighted for his services. Again the liner returned to her original role and for 14 years had an uneventful career. However, disaster struck in July 1968 when a fire started in the officers' smoke room while she was 300 miles east of New Zealand. The blaze spread rapidly, destroying the radio room. For three days the crew fought the flames and managed to save the ship, but seven lives were lost. *Gothic* limped back to Britain and did one final round trip carrying only cargo before going to the breakers in Taiwan.

Velutina *passing North Shields Fish Quay. In the background can be seen the RNVR drill ship* Satellite.

Velutina

(Completed 1950, Wallsend yard). Swan Hunter and Wigham Richardson were often at the forefront of oil tanker design and they became the lead company in constructing a new breed of large tankers that the Anglo Saxon Petroleum Company (Shell) of London ordered in 1948. One of these was *Velutina*. This sea mammoth was to carry 28,000 tons of oil. Today a ship of this size would be regarded as no more than a 'tramping' tanker, but at the time of her completion she was the largest such vessel to be built in the UK. The ship was launched into the Tyne on April 4 1950 by Princess Margaret. It was the first post-war royal launch on the river. *Velutina* served in the oil trade for 21 years before being converted into a floating workshop and crane barge, being renamed *Champion*.

Ian Rae

Leda

(Completed 1953, Wallsend yard). Launched by Princess Astrid of Norway in September 1952, this liner served on the ferry service between the Tyne and Bergen for 21 years. She was built with accommodation for 500 passengers and was the first North Sea ferry to be fitted with stabilisers. In 1977 her owners, the Bergen Line, sold her and she became an accommodation ship for workers at a Norwegian shipyard. This role continued after *Leda* was again sold, this time to Kuwaiti owners. In 1981 she was bought by a Greek company who modernised her at Piraeus to become a cruise ship. She has so far served under six names and owners, cruising in the waters of the Mediterranean, North and South America and Africa. After 40 years of service she now sails as *Star of Venice*.

When the boat comes in – Leda approaches the Tyne Commission Quay at North Shields after a voyage from Norway.

Philipson Studios, Newcastle upon Tyne

Bergensfjord, *Norway bound, leaving the Tyne on her delivery voyage.*

Bergensfjord

(Completed 1956, Wallsend yard). Launched in July 1955 by Princess Astrid of Norway, the elegant passenger ship *Bergensfjord* was built for service with the Norwegian America Line. She was delivered to her owners in Oslo in May 1956, arriving on Norwegian Independence Day to a warm welcome. She served on the Oslo-Copenhagen-New York route, but was also used increasingly for cruising to such areas as the West Indies and Mediterranean. In 1971 *Bergensfjord* was sold to the French Line and renamed *De Grasse*. She was placed on the line's Le Havre-Caribbean service and was also used as a cruise ship. In 1974 she was sold again, this time to Singapore owners and became a cruise liner in Asian waters under the name *Rasa Sayang*. Later came two more changes of ownership. However, the ship's career was abruptly ended in May 1980 while she was being given a refit at the Perama yard, Piraeus, Greece. A fire broke out in the *Rasa Sayang*'s engine room and spread, causing extensive damage. She was towed to Kynosoura where the wreck capsized. It was a sad ending for a fine liner.

Philipson Studios, Newcastle upon Tyne

Clan Finlay

(Completed 1962, Wallsend yard). Five cargo ships were ordered from Wallsend by the Clan Line in 1960-61. A typical cargo liner of the time, *Clan Finlay* had her engines positioned aft and four of the five holds were placed forward of the bridge.

One was served by an 80-ton lift derrick. The ship was powered by Sulzer diesel engines. *Clan Finlay* and her sisters maintained a monthly service between Liverpool and the Gulf. She was eventually sold to Iranian owners in 1968.

Both Philipson Studios, Newcastle upon Tyne

Lobito Palm *at sea (inset) and three of her earlier sisters under construction at the Neptune yard.*

Lobito Palm

(Completed 1960, Neptune yard). Between 1955 and 1965 the Neptune yard produced 17 cargo ships of similar design for the Europe-West Africa service. A dozen of these were built for Unilever's Palm Line with its distinctive green funnel and palm tree logo. These vessels were generally engaged on an 80-day round trip, calling at up to 20 ports. *Lobito Palm* was born in the days when modern fabrication techniques were first being tried out and she was constructed in only 34 weeks. Four years earlier a sister ship had taken over 12 months to complete using older methods.

Power and elegance – the Neptune-built Vistafjord *passing North Shields on her way to speed trials.*

Vistafjord

(Completed 1973, Neptune yard). This magnificent vessel has the honour of being the last passenger liner launched on the Tyne. Originally built for the Norwegian-America Line, the *Vistafjord* was sold to Britain's prestigious Cunard company in 1983, given a major refit in Malta, and is now a world-acclaimed luxury cruise liner. She has specially strengthened bows as a precaution against ice when she cruises in the Arctic waters of the North Cape of Norway and Spitzbergen. Her maximum speed is around 22.5 knots, but her normal cruising rate is 20.

Ian Rae

HMS Bristol *returning to the Tyne after trials.*

HMS *Bristol*

(Completed 1973, Neptune yard). This unique destroyer was the largest warship launched from the Neptune slipways. She was to have been the first of a class of warships designed as long-range escorts for aircraft carriers, but the scheme was abandoned and no other destroyers like *Bristol* were built. This one-off vessel was used as a trials ship for the Vickers MK8 automatic 4.5 inch naval gun, the Sea Dart guided weapons system and the Anglo Australian Ikara anti-submarine missile. In November 1974 *Bristol* was badly damaged by a fire and flooding in two of the engine rooms. The repairs took three years to complete and cost £8 million. In 1982 the destroyer was part of the second wave of ships to be sent to the Falklands conflict. By 1987 she had become a training ship for officer cadets at Dartmouth.

Ian Rae

Esso Northumbria *leaving the Tyne on her delivery voyage in February 1970.*

Esso Northumbria

(Completed 1970, Wallsend yard). This oil-carrying giant is well remembered by Tynesiders. The eight supertankers built at Wallsend between 1968 and 1976 were the largest vessels ever born on the river. Launched by Princess Anne in May 1969, *Esso Northumbria* was the first down the slipways. The relative narrowness of the Tyne meant that the supertanker had to be launched diagonally into the river and to allow more space a section of the opposite bank, at Hebburn, was removed. Not surprisingly, thousands turned up to watch the launch. *Esso Northumbria* could carry 252,000 tonnes of oil – 70 million gallons. The ship's primary route was from the Gulf to Fawley, near Southampton. After a career lasting only 12 years she was broken up in Taiwan.

Ark Royal is towed down the Tyne by tugs for her delivery voyage.

HMS *Ark Royal*

(Completed 1985, launched at Wallsend, fitted out at Swan's Walker Naval yard, formerly owned by Vickers Armstrong). This modern day aircraft carrier epitomises the pride of the Tyneside shipbuilding industry and its lasting relationship with the Royal Navy. *Ark Royal*, the fifth RN ship to bear the famous name, was launched at Wallsend by the Queen Mother in June 1981. She was ready for sea trials by October 1984 and was delivered the following year. Her sister, HMS *Illustrious*, was completed by Swan Hunter in 1982. Both ships are powered by gas turbine engines and their aircraft include the famous Sea Harrier. They are equipped with state-of-the-art radar, sonar and weapons systems.